L/A 6|10

Please return/renew this item by the
last date shown to avoid a charge.
Books may also be renewed by phone
and Internet. May not be renewed if
required by another reader.
**www.libraries.barnet.gov.uk**

**LONDON BOROUGH**

Remember the days of old, consider the years of many generations:
Ask thy father, and he will declare unto thee: Thine elders, and they will tell thee.
Deuteronomy XXX11 v.7                               דברים לב ז

Published by
The Jewish Genealogical Society of Great Britain
Registered Charity No. 1022738
JGSGB Publications, PO Box 180, St. Albans,
Hertfordshire, AL2 3WH, England
email: publications@jgsgb.org.uk
website: www.jgsgb.org.uk


First edition  May 2007

ISBN: 978-0-9551023-0-1


Front cover designed by
Rosemary Hoffman and Derek Wenzerul


Printed and bound in the United Kingdom
by the Alden Group, Witney, Oxon. OX29 OYG
☎ 01993 707360

# CONTENTS

# JEWISH GENEALOGICAL SOCIETY OF GREAT BRITAIN (JGSGB)

The JGSGB is the premier Society for Jewish genealogy in Great Britain. It encourages genealogical research and promotes the preservation of Jewish genealogical records and resources. It also provides a forum where members can share their information.

Both beginners and experienced genealogists, whether Jewish or not, are welcome to join the Society. Members have the opportunity to meet like-minded people in central London as well as at meetings of our regional groups in the Chilterns, East London, Leeds, Manchester, Oxford, the South Coast, and South-west London.

## GENERAL ENQUIRIES
For enquiries on family research, write to The Enquiries Officer, JGSGB, 33 Seymour Place, London W1H 5AP or email: **enquiries@jgsgb.org.uk** The Society's website, **www.jgsgb.org.uk** has a resource-packed section with links to most other genealogical websites.

## MEMBERSHIP ENQUIRIES
Membership Secretary, PO Box 42780, London N2 0YH, England. Email: **membership@jgsgb.org.uk**

## LIBRARY AND RESOURCE CENTRE
In 2006 this moved to new premises at 33 Seymour Place, London W1H 5AP. The Centre contains extensive information and genealogical resources, including several hundred reference books and a large collection of maps and leaflets. It also holds microfilms and microfiches, including copies of many of the major Anglo-Jewish genealogy collections and a large number of *Yizkor* (Memorial) books. The Society has computers with Internet access and a selection of genealogical CD-ROMs and other genealogical databases. Volunteers are on hand to assist members. For opening times contact the Society.

## - BEGINNERS

Family history workshops and computer courses are held from time to time and a one-to-one mentoring scheme is available, putting beginners in touch with more experienced researchers who can try to point them in the right direction.

## - EXPERIENCED RESEARCHERS

The Society holds an annual seminar and regular meetings of regional and Special Interest Groups (SIGs). Visits are sometimes made to cemeteries and to archive collections. Genealogical workshops also take place.

## - EVERYONE

Members receive a quarterly *Newsletter* which reports on regional meetings, genealogical events, useful websites and includes the programme for the following three months. A quarterly journal *Shemot* (Names) contains original articles written by members based on their own research, book reviews and reports of national and international meetings. Both publications welcome members' letters. The Society runs an online discussion group and a members-only website.

## PUBLICATIONS

The Society's books are listed at the end of this Guide as is information about ordering them. Back issues of *Shemot* are available from: Shemot, JGSGB, 33 Seymour Place, London W1H 5AP at £2.50 per copy (in the UK), £3 overseas. If you are trying to trace *Shemot* in a public library, its international reference number is ISSN 0969-2258.

# ACKNOWLEDGEMENTS

Much of the material in this Guide is drawn directly from the premier resources available to the Jewish genealogical community, in particular JewishGen, the Jewish Records Indexing Poland project (JRI) and to the films and materials in the Family History Library of the Church of Jesus Christ and Latter-day Saints (LDS).

I would like to thank the following, both for their specific and general contributions to this Guide, and acknowledge their copyright of materials in the chapters indicated where this is not otherwise acknowledged in the text.

Warren Blatt and JewishGen Inc. (Chapters 2-5)
Richard Cooper
Stanley Diamond, Mark Halpern and JRI-Poland (Chapters 6-9)
Gesher Galicia Inc.
Gary Mokotoff and Avotaynu Inc.
Judith Samson (Chapter 15 plus her invaluable editorial contribution)

Material in Chapter 13 is reprinted by permission of The Church of Jesus Christ of Latter-day Saints. In granting permission, the Church does not imply endorsement or authorisation of this publication.

**Susan Fifer**

**Susan Fifer** has been researching her family history since 1994 when she purchased a computer program and started inputting information about her mother's many cousins. Her interest in both computers and family history has continued and she pursues both actively in her retirement, teaching computer skills to older learners and remaining obsessive about genealogy. She was a Shtetl Co-Op Co-Ordinator for the town of Kalisz which produced some 28,000 entries for the JRI Poland database project, an achievement of which she is very proud. She hopes one day to complete and write up her own family history research.

**Rosemary Wenzerul**
Chairman, JGSGB Publications Committee
Member of Council

# INTRODUCTION

A significant amount of the Jewish genealogical material available worldwide is focused on Poland, home to millions of Jews until the Second World War. This is reflected in the large number of researchers who have one or more ancestors from this area.

Before 1772, Poland (more correctly the Poland-Lithuania Commonwealth) was the largest country in Europe. This area included all or parts of the current countries of Poland, Lithuania, Latvia, Estonia, Russia, Belarus, Ukraine and Moldova. The changing boundaries of Eastern Europe in the 19th and 20th centuries are a recurring theme in Jewish genealogy. The JGSGB has already published separate guides on Lithuania and Latvia/Estonia. This Guide is focused primarily on the area known as Congress or Russian Poland with additional sections about Galicia, Prussian Poland and the Bialystok area which was part of the Russian Pale of Settlement. Much of the general information on research, reading records and planning trips applies to all these areas.

The Guide aims to serve as an introduction to basic resources and concepts and to point researchers in the right direction. It cannot be as comprehensive as many of the excellent publications already available both in printed form and on the Internet and for this reason does not include detailed information on specific towns.

Recent years have seen a significant increase in the use of the Internet as a tool for family historians. This Guide has an emphasis on information, databases and resources which are accessible through the Internet. It is possible, of course, to undertake research by personally visiting libraries and archives, by writing letters and making phone calls. For many researchers of Jewish genealogy, however, the broad geographical scope involved in searching for their ancestors can make this a time-consuming and costly process. Increasingly libraries and archives have computers available to the public, and staff are usually very willing to help. Many libraries, archives and genealogical societies run courses on how to use computers and the Internet for family history research.

*Unknown Warsaw couple (courtesy Judith Samson)*

# 1
# HOW TO START YOUR RESEARCH

The two major things that you will be looking for will be the **names of individuals** and the **names of places** from which your ancestors came. If you have fairly common Jewish surnames and all you know is that they came from "somewhere in Russia or Poland," then the work can seem very difficult.

You should see yourself as a detective, trying to wring the most information from seemingly unpromising clues and sources. If you aren't lucky enough to have been given the names of towns at the beginning of your research, don't give up. There may be information available in the country in which you are living and where, presumably, your first ancestral immigrants from Poland settled.

As with all genealogical research, start with more recent records and work backwards. If you still have relatives living who were born in Poland or whose older siblings were born there, interview them first before spending time looking at archives and databases.

**Family papers and letters**

Are there letters or postcards received from relatives who were still living in their Polish town or village? If you don't have these papers, check with cousins and their families. Family papers often end up with unmarried children who stayed at home to look after their parents. Where might these papers have gone when these children themselves died?

As well as letters, there may be copies of passports and travel documents. Even if your ancestors didn't have copies of their birth certificates when they first arrived, they may have written later to the authorities in Poland when they wanted to get naturalised and needed such documentation.

## Photographs

Before camera use became widespread and relatively cheap, most photographs were taken professionally. People often had these printed on postcards and sent them to relatives, sweethearts and friends. If there are original family photographs from Poland, look to see if the name of a photographer and/or town is included in the information on the back or at the bottom of the picture.

*Photographer's details on reverse of family photograph*
*(courtesy Judith Samson)*

Our ancestors often used a variety of names at different times and for different purposes. Even today, most Jews still have both secular and Hebrew names. Many of us use nicknames or shortened versions of our given names. Professionals such as singers, writers and actors may use different names. We should therefore not be surprised if our ancestors also played the 'alternative name game,' however frustrating this may be for our research. An interesting article on this subject is *Alternate Surnames in Russian Poland* by Lauren B. Eisenberg Davis which can be found at:
**www.JewishGen.org/InfoFiles/pl-sname.html**

Fixed family names only became common at the beginning of the 19th century in Poland, usually as a result of legislation. Research before this time has to rely on first/given name traditions such as naming children after a deceased grandparent or other relative.

## Town names

If you do not already know where your ancestors came from, one of the best sources for this information is on **naturalisation records**. Of course, not everyone got naturalised. If a woman married someone who was already naturalised or who was born in the UK, for example, then she might have become a citizen without going through the process of naturalisation.

There may be time restrictions relating to the release of naturalisation papers. Depending on the country where you live, you can sometimes ask for these papers to be released early, particularly if you can show a close relationship with the person and/or the fact that they are deceased.

For those who were not naturalised, there may be UK **Exemption from Internment Certificates** from the Second World War which give the birthplace of an individual. These can be seen at the National Archives at **www.movinghere.org.uk/browse/f.htm**

In the UK, there are no centralised lists of **immigrant arrivals**. If you know that part of your family went to the United States, then you may find the name of a town by checking the names of cousins and siblings on records such as those held at Ellis Island (**www.ellisisland.org**). This can help you to narrow your search if documentary evidence is limited elsewhere.

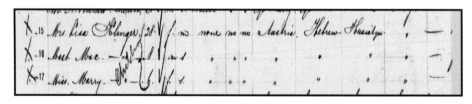

*Passenger list from Rotterdam to New York, June 1905, showing the Klinger family coming from the town of Husiatyn in Austria (Galicia)*

(A.)

NATURALIZATION ACTS, 1870.

Certificate of Naturalization to an Alien.

HOME OFFICE, LONDON.

WHEREAS

*Barnett Milstein*

an Alien, now residing at

*2 Vine Court*
*Whitechapel, London*

has presented to me, the Right Honourable *Herbert Henry Asquith* one of Her Majesty's Principal Secretaries of State, a Memorial, praying for a Certificate of Naturalization, and alleging that he is a

*subject of Russia, having been born at Biala in Poland; and is the son of Abraham and Sophea Milstein, both subjects of Russia = of the age of Forty years = a Tailor = is married and has nine children under age residing with him vz.:-*

| | | |
|---|---|---|
| Abraham | Milstein | aged 19 years |
| Lipman | " | " 16 " |
| Rachel | " | " 12 " |
| Selina | " | " 8 " |
| Harris | " | " 7 " |
| Morris | " | " 6 " |
| Phillip | " | " 4 " |
| Esther | " | " 20 months |
| Dorah | " | " 2 " |

*Naturalisation Certificate (1895) of Barnett Milstein showing his birthplace as Biala in Poland*

Family members may have stopped off in other countries on their journey from Poland and the records of these countries may also provide important clues about places of origin. If you have exhausted all the obvious places to look, then start to think laterally.

**Census records** may give the name of a town although, in the UK, anything more than Russia, Poland or Russian Poland should be regarded as a bonus.

Some **gravestones** and/or **burial records** may indicate that the deceased was a member of a burial society whose name may be an indication of the area in which they were born.

One means of trying to link towns with particular names is to look in Alexander Beider's book *A Dictionary of Jewish Surnames from the Kingdom of Poland*. This lists surnames and towns where significant numbers of those names appear. While this is not infallible, it is a useful place to start if you have no other clues to help you.

Town names may change over time depending on the administration and geopolitical circumstances operating (see Chapter 2 on Basic history and geography). A number of sources may help you to find a town including the *Index of German-Polish and Polish-German names of the localities in Poland & Russia* at **www.atsnotes.com/other/gerpol.html**

Other useful sources about town names include: *Where Once We Walked: A Guide to the Jewish Communities Destroyed in the Holocaust* by Gary Mokotoff and Sallyann Sack which identifies over 6000 Polish towns. Each entry gives latitude/longitude, Jewish population before the Holocaust and cites related reference books.

The pages of testimony at **Yad Vashem** (Israel's memorial to Holocaust victims) can be a major source of information to those trying to follow up the fate of family members who were living in Poland during the Second World War. This database can be searched by name and/or location at **www.yadvashem.org/lwp/workplace/IY_HON_Welcome**

*Yizkor* (**memorial) books**) were written by groups of former residents, or *Landsmanshaften*, and published as a tribute to their homes and the people who were murdered during the Holocaust. The majority of these books were written in Hebrew or Yiddish. The *Yizkor* book project **www.JewishGen.org/Yizkor/** aims to translate many of these into English. The JGSGB library has an extensive collection of *Yizkor* books and the Society has published a volume listing their locations in the UK.

**ShtetlSeeker** is a facility which allows you to look for towns either by name or by location. If searching by name you can use the **soundex** function which lets you find towns which sound the same as the town you are seeking. This is very useful if you don't know the exact spelling of the town, if you only have a vague recollection of the town name or if the spelling you are using has been anglicised and is not in use in modern Poland. Soundex can also be used in surname searches on Jewish genealogical websites. ShtetlSeeker can be searched on the JewishGen website at **www.JewishGen.org/ShtetlSeeker/**

# ShtetlSeeker – Town Search

Search for **town** Kalisz in Central/Eastern Europe.

Narrow the search by **country**?: All Countries (31) ▼

Measure distances in: ⊙ Miles ○ Kilometers

Show the distance and direction from:
⊙ The capital city of the relevant country
○ Latitude: [ ]° [ ]' Longitude: [ ]° [ ]'.
○ Selected City: Select Country ▼ No cities ▼

Search method: Sounds Like – Daitch-Mokotoff Soundex ▼

Start the search

*Search screen from ShtetlSeeker*

14

| Modern Town & Country | Other Names | c. 1950 After WWII Town / Country | c. 1930 Between Wars Town / District / Province / Country | c. 1900 Before WWI Town / District / Province / Country | # of JGFF Entries |
|---|---|---|---|---|---|
| Kalisz, Poland 51°45' 18°05' 207 km WSW of Warszawa | Kalisz [Pol], Kalisch [Ger], Kalish [Rus, Yid], Calisia [Lat], Kolish | Kalisz <br><br> Poland | Kalisz Kalisz Łódź Poland | Kalisz Kalisz Kalisz Russian Empire | 561 |
| | | Kielce | Kielce | Kielce | |

*Results screen from the Jewish Communities search function on ShtetlSeeker. This gives a smaller range of towns which were likely to have had a Jewish population. It also shows the number of entries registered for this town on the JGFF (Jewish Genealogical Family Finder.)*

Once you have the geographical co-ordinates for your town you should widen your research. Although your ancestors may have lived in a small place, they may have registered events such as births, marriages and deaths in the nearest large town.

One significant resource which can help your search for records, towns, names and research methodology is the international Jewish genealogical community itself. Contact individual researchers who are researching the same towns, even if they don't share any of your family names. There is no point in going to time, trouble and expense to look for or access records if others have already done this work and can give you tips to help or speed up your research.

Leave the names and towns that you are researching on the **Jewish Genealogical Family Finder** (JGFF). You will need to register to do this but registration is free at **www.JewishGen.org/jgff/** You will then be able to look for researchers with similar interests to your own and also to leave your details so that others can find you.

Join a SIG (**Special Interest Group**). There may be one within your own national genealogical society - we have several in JGSGB. Many researchers communicate with each other on the Internet and exchange emails and information through this medium.

The JewishGen website has links to the following groups at
**www.JewishGen.org/InfoFiles/#Poland**

- Danzig/Gdańsk SIG
- Gesher Galicia SIG (Austrian Poland)
- Jewish Records Indexing Poland (JRI)
- Suwałki-Łomża *gubernias* SIG - *Landsmen* journal
- Kielce-Radom *gubernias* SIG
- Warszawa (Warsaw) Research Group

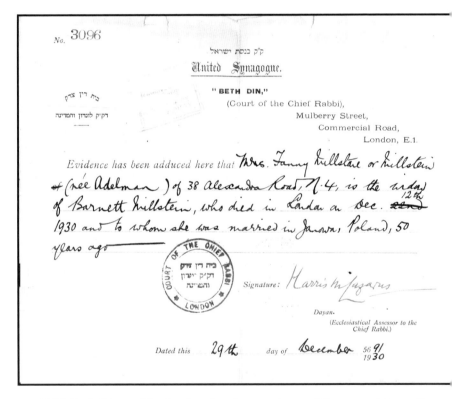

*1930 Beth Din certificate showing the marriage of Fanny and Barnett Millstein as taking place in Janowa, Poland c1880*

# 2
# BASIC HISTORY AND GEOGRAPHY

It is generally agreed that the first written record of Jews in Poland was by a Moorish/Spanish Jew named Ibrahim ibn Jacob in 966. The early Jews who came to Poland between the 12th and 15th centuries were mainly traders. This major influx took place when the Crusades and the Inquisition led to the persecution of Jews in the countries of Western and Southern Europe.

Polish dukes and kings, such as Bolesław Pobożny (1221-1279) and Kazimierz Wielki (1310-1370) granted them privileges and a significant measure of self-government. Pobożny's Charter of Kalisz (1264) guaranteed full security for Jews, their communities, and property.

Poland and Lithuania combined in 1569. This large country now had about 80% of world Jewry living in relative peace, with religious freedom and governed by the Council of the Four Lands. Although there were anti-semitic incidents and laws, the relative freedom of Jews living in most areas of the Commonwealth is often stressed. The golden age of Polish Jewry lasted into the 18th century, when the Commonwealth weakened and fell apart.

Between 1772 and 1795, Poland was partitioned between Russia, Austria, and Prussia, and ceased to be an independent nation for over 100 years, until it was re-established after the First World War (WWI) in 1918.

Finding genealogical records for the early period is virtually impossible unless you are descended from one of the well-known rabbinic families whose family trees were well documented and preserved. Most genealogical records to which researchers have access date from the beginning of the 19th century and it is therefore on the political, geographical and administrative systems of this period that this Guide will focus.

## Important dates

- **1795** Third and final partition of Poland; Poland ceases to exist as a nation. Northern and western areas (Poznań, Kalisz, Warsaw, Łomża, Białystok) taken by Prussia; Eastern areas (Vilna, Grodno, Brest) taken by Russia; Southern areas (Kielce, Radom, Lublin, Siedlce) become part of Austrian province of West Galicia.

- **1807** Duchy of Warsaw created by Napoleon, from former Prussian partition territory.

- **1809** Napoleon defeats Austria; Western Galicia, including most of the future Kielce, Radom, Lublin and Siedlce *gubernias* (provinces), becomes part of Duchy of Warsaw.

- **1815** Napoleon defeated; Congress of Vienna; "Kingdom of Poland" formed from former Duchy of Warsaw, now under Russian control.

- **1863** Kingdom of Poland: Insurrection against Russia.

- **1918** End of World War I: Treaty of Versailles. Poland reborn as a nation.

Between 1918 and 1939, newly independent Poland included parts of the Russian *gubernias* of Vilna, Grodno and Volhynia; the Austrian province of Galicia; Prussian Poznań and West Prussia.

After WWII, nearly half of inter-war Poland (its eastern provinces: Wilno, Nowogródek, Polesie, Wołyń, Tarnopol, Stanisławów and parts of Lwów and Białystok) became part of the Soviet Union — these areas are now part of Ukraine, Belarus and Lithuania. Poland gained former German areas: most of Pommern (Pomerania), Brandenburg, Schlesien (Silesia), West Prussia, and half of East Prussia.

The maps in this Guide give some idea of the complex changes that took place in the area which we now know as Poland and are reproduced from *A Dictionary of Jewish Surnames from the Kingdom of Poland* by kind permission of Avotaynu Inc.

A useful map of modern Poland can be found at **http://mapa.szukacz.pl/** which allows you to look at an outline of Poland and then zoom in to street level in larger towns. You can also 'click and drag' the map to move around the country. Double-clicking on any part of the map makes that the centre of your search.

## Gazetteers and directories

The gazetteer (*Słownik Geograficzny Królestwa Polskiego i innych krajów słowiańskich*) published between 1880 and 1902, is very useful for finding places in Poland. Coverage includes all localities in the former Polish provinces of Russia, most localities in the former

Austrian province of Galicia (now divided between Poland and the Ukraine). Some entries have been translated. Information on this resource can be found at:
**www.polishroots.com/slownik/slownik_geograficzny.htm**
A set of these can also be found at the Royal Geographical Society in London: **www.rgs.org**

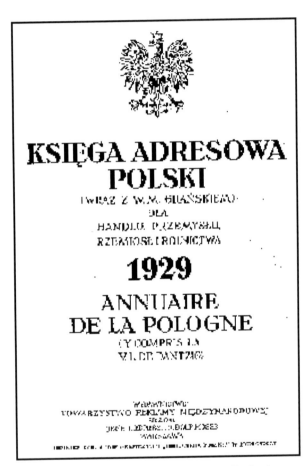

*1929 Polish Business Directory Project*
*Jewish Records Indexing - Poland*
*in cooperation with Jewishgen*
***www.jewishgen.org/JRI-PL/bizdir/start.htm***

3

# HISTORY OF BIRTH, MARRIAGE AND DEATH RECORDS

Civil vital registration (birth, marriage and death records) in what became Russian Poland (the Kingdom of Poland, also known as Congress Poland) began in 1808 in the Duchy of Warsaw, and the records were kept in "Napoleonic format", a paragraph-essay style.

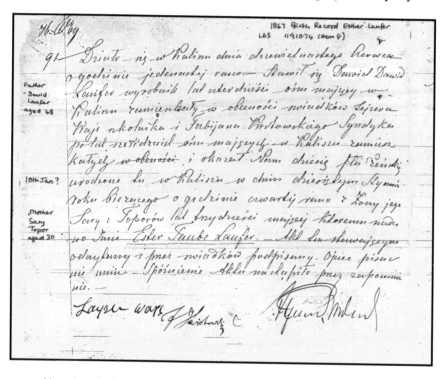

*Napoleonic (narrative) format birth record of Ester Taube Laufer (great-grandmother of the author) Kalisz, 1867*

Records were kept in the Polish language from 1808 until 1868, and thereafter in Russian, until 1918, when Poland regained its independence.

# RECORD-KEEPING

This depends upon the occupying power: Russian, Austria, Prussia.

## Russian Poland (Kingdom of Poland)

- **1808** Civil registration was established by Napoleon; Jews and others were included in Catholic civil registers. In some larger towns, however, separate Jewish registers may exist from this date. These records are in Polish.

- **1821** Jews were required to take surnames - Russian government mandate. Again, in larger towns, surnames would have been common from much earlier.

- **1826** Separate registers were now introduced for each religious community - Roman Catholic, Jewish, Russian Orthodox, Protestant, etc. These records are also in Polish.

- **1868** Record-keeping switches from Polish to Russian.

## An overview of Jewish vital records in Russian Poland[1]

| Years | 1808 - 1825 | 1826 - 1867 | 1868 - 1917 | 1918 - 1942 |
|---|---|---|---|---|
| **Where recorded** | Catholic civil transcripts | Separate Jewish registers | | |
| **Language** | Polish | | Russian | Polish |
| **Location of Registers** | | Records older than 100 years are kept in regional branches of the Polish State Archives. Many of these records have been microfilmed by the Mormons, usually up to around 1865 or later for some towns. | Records less than 100 years old are typically kept in each town's Civil Records Office (*Urząd Stanu Cywilnego*). | |

[1] This chart applies only to records in localities within the semi-autonomous region under Russian rule known as the Kingdom of Poland (Congress Poland, also known as Russian Poland). The area covered forms almost half of present-day Poland. For other localities which are now part of Poland (eg former parts of Galicia, Prussian Poland, Grodno *Gubernia*), the record format, language, and periods covered are different.

- **1810** Duchy of Warsaw: Civil vital registration begins in former West Galicia (includes Kielce-Radom-Lublin-Siedlce region).

*Kraków Archives (© Judith Samson)*

# 4
# ADMINISTRATIVE DIVISIONS

During its history, the internal subdivisions of Russian Poland were changed several times. Listed below are the major geographical administrative subdivisions since 1807.

**1807** Napoleon's Duchy of Warsaw (in Polish *Księstwo Warszawskie)* was divided into six *départements*: Varsovie (Warschau), Posen, Kalisz, Bromberg, Płock, and Łomża.

**1809** Napoleon defeated the Austrians and took the Austrian territory from the third partition, expanding the Duchy of Warsaw and adding the four *départements* of Krakovie (Krakau), Radom, Lublin and Siedlce.

**1815** The Kingdom of Poland, now part of the Russian Empire, was divided into **eight** *województwa*. Each *województwo* (province) was divided into *obwód* (districts), which were in turn subdivided into *powiat* (sub-districts).

1  **Augustów**: later Suwałki *gubernia* (province) + Łomża-Kolno-Szczuczyn-Tykocin districts.

2  **Kalisz:** later Kalisz *gubernia* + Piotrków.

3  **Kraków:** later Kielce *gubernia* + Będzin.  Despite its name, the city of Kraków, independent until 1846, was not included;

4  **Lublin:** later Lublin *gubernia*.

5  **Mazowsze:** (Mazovia) later Warszawa *gubernia* + Łęczyca, Rawa, Brzeziny and Łódż districts.

6  **Płock:** later Płock *gubernia* + Ostrołęka-Maków-Ostrów-Pułtusk-Płońsk districts.

7  **Podlesie:** (Podlasia) later Siedlce *gubernia*.

8  **Sandomierz:** later Radom *gubernia*.

Baltic Sea

Königsberg

Mariampol

The Kingdom
of Poland
(1815-1844)

Suwałki
Augustów

RUSSIA

PRUSSIA

Mława
PŁOCK  Ostrołęka  Łomża
Pułtusk
Włocławek  Płock

MAZOVIA
Warsaw  Siedlce
Kalisz  Luków  Biała
PODLASIA
Piotrków  Radom
KALISZ  SANDOMIERZ  Lublin
Kielce  Sandomierz  LUBLIN
Będzin  Janów
KRAKOW

Kraków

AUSTRIA

Copyright © 1996 by Avotaynu, Inc.

**1844** The *województwa* were abolished and replaced with **five** *gubernia*s. Each was divided into several *powiat* (districts):

1     **Warszawa:** formed from Kalisz and Mazowsze *województwa*. Contains *powiat*s of Warszawa, Gostynin, Kujawski, Sochaczew, Stanisławów, Łęczyca, Rawa, Kalisz, Konin, Sieradz, Wieluń and Piotrków.

2     **Augustów:** same territory as former Augustów *województwo*. Capital is Suwałki. Contains *powiat*s of Augustów, Sejny, Kalwaria, Mariampol and Łomża.

3     **Płock:** same territory as former Płock *województwo*. Contains *powiat*s of Płock, Lipno, Mława, Przasnysz, Pułtusk and Ostrołęka.

25

4    **Radom:** formed from Sandomierz and Kraków *województwa*. Contains *powiat*s of Radom, Opatów, Opoczno, Sandomierz, Kielce, Miechów, Olkusz and Stopnica.

5    **Lublin:** formed from Lublin and Podlesie *województwa*. Contains *powiat*s of Lublin, Krasnystaw, Zamość, Hrubieszów, Siedlce, Łuków, Biała and Radzyń.

**1867** The *gubernia* subdivisions were changed, with the Kingdom divided into **ten** *gubernia*s, each subdivided into *powiat*s of which there was a total of 84.

1    **Kalisz:** part of former Warszawa *gubernia*. *Powiat*s: Słupca, Konin, Koło, Turek, Łęczyca, Kalisz, Sieradz, Wieluń.

2    **Kielce:** part of former Radom *gubernia*. *Powiat*s: Kielce, Włoszczowa, Jędrzejów, Pińczów, Stopnica, Miechów, Olkusz.

3    **Łomża:** parts of former Augustów and Płock *gubernia*s. *Powiat*s: Szczuczyn, Kolno, Łomża, Ostrołęka, Pułtusk (not shown on map opposite), Maków, Mazowieck, Ostrów.

4    **Lublin:** part of former Lublin *gubernia*. *Powiat*s: Puławy, Lubartów, Lublin, Chełm, Krasnystaw, Janów, Hrubieszów, Zamość, Biłgoraj, Tomaszów.

5    **Piotrków:** part of former Warszawa *gubernia*. *Powiat*s: Łódź, Brzeziny, Rawa, Łask, Piotrków, Nowo-Radomsk, Częstochowa, Będzin.

6    **Płock:** part of former Płock *gubernia*. *Powiat*s: Rypin, Lipno, Sierpc, Płock, Mlawa, Płońsk, Przasnysz, Ciechanów.

7    **Radom:** part of former Radom *gubernia*. *Powiat*s: Kozienice, Radom, Opoczno, Końskie, Iłża, Opatów, Sandomierz.

8    **Siedlce:** part of former Lublin *gubernia*. *Powiat*s: Sokołów, Węgrów, Konstatynów, Biała Podlaska, Siedlce, Łuków, Garwolin, Radzyń, Włodawa.

The Kingdom
of Poland at the
Beginning of the
20th Century

Baltic Sea

Kovno

Königsberg

Władysławów
Wyłkowyszki

Danzig
(Gdansk)

Mariampol
Kalwaria

EAST
PRUSSIA

SUWAŁKI
Sejny

WEST
PRUSSIA

Suwałki

Augustów

Grodno

Szczuczyn
Kolno

POSEN

Posen
(Poznań)

Rypin
Lipno
Sierpc
Nieszawa
Włocławek
Słupca
Gostynin
Konin
Koło
Turek
Łęczyca

PRUSSIA

ŁOMŻA

Mława Przasnysz
Ciechanów
Ostrołęka
Łomża

Białystok

PŁOCK

Maków
Mazowieck

Płock
Płońsk
Pułtusk
Ostrów

RUSSIAN
EMPIRE

WARSAW

Kutno
Sochaczew
Radzymin
Sokołów
Wegrów

Błonie
Łowicz
Skierniewice
Warsaw
Nowo Mińsk
Siedlce
Konstantynów

KALISZ

Kalisz

Biała
Brest

Grójec
Garwolin

Łuków
SIEDLCE

Sieradz
Łódź
Brzeziny
Łask
Rawa

Kozienice
Radzyń

Wieluń

Piotrków
Opoczno
Radom
Konskie

Puławy
Lubartów
Włodawa

RADOM

PIOTRKÓW

Nowo
Radomsk
Częstochowa

Włoszczowa

Iłza

Lublin

LUBLIN

Chełm

Kielce
Opatów
Sandomierz
Krasnystaw

KIELCE

Jędrzejów
Janów
Hrubieszów
Zamość
Lutsk

Będzin
Pińczów
Bilgoraj
Tomaszów

SILESIA

Olkusz
Miechów
Stopnica

Krakau (Kraków)

GALICIA

Lemberg (Lwów)

9    **Suwałki:** part of former Augustów *gubernia*. *Powiat*s: Władysławów, Wyłkowyszki, Mariampol, Kalwaria, Sejny, Suwałki, Augustów.

10   **Warszawa:** part of former Warszawa *gubernia*. *Powiat*s: Nieszawa, Włocławek, Gostynin, Kutno, Łowicz, Skierniewice, Błonie, Sochaczew, Radzymin, Warszawa, Nowo-Mińsk, Grójec.

These *gubernia* borders were stable until the end of the Kingdom of Poland during WWI (1917). It is these ten *gubernias* to which genealogists typically refer, since this was the period during which the majority of our ancestors emigrated from Poland.

**1918**    Poland became an independent nation for the first time in over 120 years. The territory of inter-war Poland was much larger than the pre-1917 Russian Kingdom of Poland, gaining territories from the former Russian, Prussian and Austro-Hungarian Empires.

Poland was divided into **16** *województwas*, which were in turn each divided into several *powiat*s (districts): Warszawa, Łódź, Kielce, Lublin, Białystok, Nowogródek, Polesie, Wołyn, Poznań, Pomorze, Kraków, Lwów, Stanisławów, Tarnopol, Śląsk, Wilno

**1945**    After WWII, Poland's borders changed dramatically — the entire country moved west. It gained former German areas in the west, and lost much eastern territory to the USSR (inter-war provinces of Wilno, Nowogródek, Podlasie, Wołyn, Lwów, Stanisławów and Tarnopol).

Poland was divided into **17** *województwas*: Szczecin, Koszalin, Gdańsk, Olsztyn, Zielona Góra, Wrocław, Poznań, Bydgoszcz, Opole, Katowice, Łódź, Warszawa, Białystok, Kielce, Kraków, Lublin and Rzeszów.

These provinces were used until 1975, and are significant for genealogical research because these are the provinces which the LDS Family History Library Catalogue uses to classify all records of Poland.

**1975** Poland's internal provinces were realigned, with the former 17 provinces becoming 49.

**1999** Poland's internal provinces were realigned again, reducing the number of *województwas* from 49 to 16

| Province *województwo* | Adjectival form | Capital city |
|---|---|---|
| Dolny Śląsk | Dolnośląskie | Wrocław |
| Kujawy-Pomorze | kujawsko-pomorskie | Bydgoszcz & Torun |
| Lubusz | Lubuskie | Gorzów & Zielona Gora |
| Łódź | Łódzkie | Łódź |
| Lublin | Lubelskie | Lublin |
| Mazowsze | Mazowieckie | Warszawa |
| Małopolska | Małopolskie | Kraków |
| Opole | Opolskie | Opole |
| Podlasie | Podlaskie | Białystok |
| Podkarpacie | Podkarpackie | Rzeszów |
| Pomorze | Pomorskie | Gdańsk |
| Śląsk | Śląskie | Katowice |
| Święty Krzyż | Świętokrzyskie | Kielce |
| Warmia i Mazury | warmińsko-mazurskie | Olsztyn |
| Wielkopolska | Wielkopolskie | Poznań |
| Pomorze Zachodnie | zachodniopomorskie | Szczecin |

# WHAT RECORDS ARE AVAILABLE?

Generally, vital records (birth, marriage and death records) under 100 years old are still held in each town's civil registration office (*Urząd Stanu Cywilnego - USC*), while records over 100 years old are at one of the **Polish State Archives (PSA)** regional branches.

There are surviving Jewish vital records for over 600 Polish towns. To see what Jewish vital records are available for each town, consult the following resources:

- Polish Archive Holdings of Jewish Vital Records, by Town showing which branch of the PSA holds Jewish vital records for each town. A list can be seen at:

**www.JewishGen.org/InfoFiles/Poland/PolishTownsArchives.htm**

- ***Jewish Roots in Poland: Pages from the Past and Archival Inventories***, by Miriam Weiner contains a detailed inventory of Jewish records at all PSA branches and USC offices. It can also be seen online at **www.rtrfoundation.org**

- ***Księgi metrykalne i stanu cywilnego w archiwach państwowych w Polsce*** (*Metrical and civil registration documents in the State Archives in Poland*) edited by Anna Laszuk. This is an inventory, in Polish, of the vital records of all religious groups held by branches of the PSA.

- **SEZAM database** is a comprehensive web-searchable database of all holdings of the Polish State Archives at **www.archiwa.gov.pl/?CIDA=177**

  This Polish database, covers all PSA holdings, of which vital records are only a small percentage. Jewish vital records are indicated by Polish terms such as *"Akta metrykalne żydowskiej"*, *"Akta Stanu Cywilnego gminy żydowskiej"*, *"Urząd Stanu Cywilnego Gminy Wyznania Mojżeszowego"*, *"Akta stanu cywilnego Okręgu Bożniczego"*

See also

**http://baza.archiwa.gov.pl/sezam/pradziad.eng.php**

- **Mormon microfilms**. The Mormons microfilmed over 2,000 reels of 19th-century Jewish vital records in the Polish State Archives mostly dating from 1808 to 1890 (dates differ from town to town). Consult the *Family History Library Catalog*™ (FHLC), online at **www.familysearch.org** An inventory of these films is downloadable from the JRI-Poland website: **www.JewishGen.org/jri-pl/jri-lds.htm**

If you can't find your town in the above inventories, it could be because the Jewish vital records were kept in a nearby town, or have been destroyed. About 50 of the 80 branches of the Polish State Archives actually have Jewish records and many have later records that have not been microfilmed by the Mormon Church.

## Vital records which are too recent to be at the PSA

The Civil Registration Offices (USC) are supposed to turn record books over to the PSA after one hundred years. However, in a small number of cases, the USCs have sent all their Jewish registers to the State Archives. When a register contains vital records spanning the 100-year mark (for example, a marriage register in use from 1896 to 1904), it will typically remain in the USC until one hundred years have passed since the last entry in the register.

By law, USCs are not allowed to make photocopies of records; they can only prepare typed extracts of a record upon request. The full documents that you're used to seeing on LDS microfilms are in their possession - but their extracts contain only the basic information.

To obtain birth, marriage and death records after about 1900, write to the USC in your town:
Urząd Stanu Cywilnego
(Your town), POLAND.Many books contain letter-writing guides that will help you frame your request to the archives.

See also the following websites:
**www.pgsa.org/PolishLetterWriting.htm**
**www.polishroots.org/genpoland/certif.htm**

*Part of the Stawiszyn death index 1865. Alphabetical (almost!) by surname. The first column is a list number; the second column is a page number. There is no individual record (Akt) number. In the third column, note the double dates, 12 days apart, for Julian and Gregorian calendars.*

USC offices are not archives and will not perform research on your behalf. They will search for records if you give them enough information to find the record in question. The way in which requests are handled varies from office to office. Mail requests are sometimes ignored, even when they are written in Polish. In many cases, the extracts will be sent to the Polish embassy or consulate nearest to you, along with an invoice for the documents. The policy for handling requests seems to vary with the individual USC manager's own interpretation of what is appropriate. Typically, extracts that are requested for legal reasons, for example, to prove a date of birth in order to collect social security benefits, will be handled on a more formal basis.

There's also a greater language barrier at USCs than at the Polish State Archives as many of the staff in small towns may not understand sufficient English to respond to your request in English.

32

# JEWISH RECORDS INDEXING (JRI) POLAND

The JRI-Poland indexing project is a wonderful example of the power that comes from researchers working co-operatively and using the Internet to share their work. The project came about when researchers accessed vital records microfilmed for the years after 1867 when they were handwritten in Cyrillic (Russian) script rather than in Polish. For the majority of genealogists, it was impossible or extremely laborious to plough through whole microfilms trying to spot family names. Even where indexes were available, this was still very time consuming and it was easy to miss or misinterpret entries. Furthermore, there was considerable duplication of effort with each researcher trawling through the records for a small group of names.

It was decided, therefore, that it would be much more productive if all the records for a town were indexed once and then for this index to be made available to all researchers. They could then home in on the names and towns that were important to them and find the relevant records much more quickly. Initially this project concentrated on the Russian language records which were so difficult for those coming across them for the first time.

The project grew and started to add Polish language records from earlier years to the database. Support was provided in two ways. Some people provided donations to allow the project to acquire photocopies of the indexes from the microfilms. Others used these photocopies to transcribe the indexes and put them into an electronic format so that they could be added to a massive online database and searched freely by researchers. Where there were no indexes on the microfilm, these were created from the records themselves.

A typical entry on the database gives the name of the town and the reference number of the LDS film. The year of the event is then shown as is the type of event (birth, marriage or death) and a record

(*Akt*) number. Where the event is a marriage, there is usually a second line for the marriage partner. The relevant LDS films can then be ordered through a local Family History Centre and the appropriate records viewed and photocopied if necessary.

| | | | | | | |
|---|---|---|---|---|---|---|
| **Kalisz B1809-92 M1809-92 D1809-83,85-92 V1821,61** Kalisz Gubernia / Poznan Province Located at 51°45′ 18°05′ Last updated December 2004 | | | | | | |
| **Surname** | **Givenname** | **Type** | **Year** | **Akt** | **Film** | **Comments** |
| FEIFER | Dawid | B | 1818 | 63 | 743141 | |
| FAYFER | Sora | D | 1819 | 25 | 743141 | |
| FAYFER | Jude Laybus | B | 1820 | 82 | 743141 | |
| FAYFER | Fogela | D | 1821 | 30 | 743142 | |
| FAYFER | Aron | B | 1822 | 10 | 743142 | |
| FAYFER | Szylem | D | 1822 | 8 | 743142 | |
| FAYFER | Ruchela | D | 1822 | 23 | 743142 | |
| FEIFER | Aaron | D | 1822 | 116 | 743142 | |

*Results from a search of the JRI-Poland database*

The scope of the JRI-Poland project continues to grow with other kinds of records being added such as business directories and from sources such as the Jewish Historical Institute in Warsaw.

**Polish State Archives**

One major JRI-Poland project was an arrangement for the Polish State Archives (PSA) to index records which were not available through the LDS collections. Most of these were for the years after 1865. Funds were raised by researchers for the indexing work which was not undertaken by volunteers but by staff of the PSA. The results were then added to the database. If your search revealed a record of interest, this could then be ordered and paid for online through a system set up by JRI-Poland and the PSA.

The advantage of this system was that researchers could order specific records with a much greater degree of confidence that these would be relevant to their research. They did not have to write 'on spec' to the archives and incur open-ended costs while the archives were searched for potential relatives. From the point of view of the archives, it meant a much more streamlined system for responding to and helping the ever-growing number of researchers with interests in Poland.

Unfortunately, in November 2006, the appointment of a new head of the Polish State Archives coincided with a decision to terminate the arrangements with the JRI project. At the time of writing, the following announcement was posted on the PSA website.

---

*The Head Office of State Archives (Naczelna Dyrekcja Archiwów Państwowych) hereby informs about the termination of cooperation with the Jewish Record Indexing Poland (JRI-PL) as of 30 November 2006 with respect to:*
*- the development of electronic indexes to public and parish civil status (BMD) registers of the Jewish faith,*
*- placing of orders for copies of civil status (BMD) records with the State Archives through the intermediation of JRI-PL-AP Order Coordination Centre.*
*Persons interested in obtaining copies of civil status records may place orders directly with the State Archives competent due to the place of preservation of civil status (BMD) registers. Information on the location of civil status registers is available at www.archiwa.gov.pl/?CIDA=378.*
*In order to place such orders, previously used JRI-PL forms (available at www.JewishGen.org/jri-pl/psa/psabasketinst.htm) may still be used, and required data collected, e.g. from the JRI-PL database (available at www.JewishGen.org/jri-pl/jriplweb.htm).*

*In the event of any difficulties connected with the performance of queries in civil status registers from the holdings of the Polish State Archives, please do not hesitate to contact:*
*Naczelna Dyrekcja Archiwów Państwowych*
*ul. Długa 6*
*00-950 Warszawa, skr. poczt. 1005*
*Fax: +48 22 831-75-63*
*or via e-mail to the address: ndap@archiwa.gov.pl*

There is obviously great disappointment about this decision. The JRI-Poland Board is working to address this situation. The online database will continue to operate, providing a finding aid and tool for researchers to identify records of interest. Other JRI-Poland projects to index records from other sources, including the LDS Microfilms of Polish Jewish records, continue as before.

## Some tips when using the database

- Assume that the name you are researching might have been spelled in a number of different ways: it may have been transliterated originally from Hebrew or Yiddish and then later into and out of Russian. The database allows you to find the name of a person or town by using the Soundex system which relies on how a word sounds rather than exactly how it is written. This may give you some results which you feel fairly confident are not your family but may also give you the chance to find those whose names are written in ways that you might not have suspected.

- The database is growing all the time so, even if you don't find anything today, keep going back to check on records which have been added. There is a facility in the database to check against all records or against those which have been added since a particular date (which you can specify.) You can now also specify searches for a particular year or range of years.

- Similarly, if you know the geographical co-ordinates of your town, you can enter these and ask the database to search other records within a specified radius from that town. This can be useful when people said they came from a large town or an area rather than mentioning the name of a small village.

- You could support the project through donations or volunteering to help with indexing. Though many people feel that they lack the skills for the latter, it is a good way of familiarising yourself with Polish records. For details on donations, contact: JRI-Poland Treasurer, c/o Sheila Salo, 5607 Greenleaf Road, Cheverly, MD 20785 (**donations@jri-poland.org**).

**7**

# GALICIA

Galicia was one of the historical provinces of Poland, especially its western part, west of the San River, traditionally called *Małopolska*, ie Little Poland, as opposed to Greater Poland around Poznań. Kraków was its most important town. The eastern part of Galicia was previously called Ruthenia. Jews from Germany came to this area in the Middle Ages.

During the Partitions of Poland in 1772 and 1795, the Austrian Empire annexed Little Poland and Ruthenia which then became Galicia.

- **1788** Austrian government mandate in Western Galicia required Jews to take surnames.

- **1815** northern regions of Galicia were ceded to Russia and became part of the Kingdom of Poland, dependent on Russia. In the 19th century Jews formed about 10% of the population of Galicia.

*Tarnów, former Mikvah (now an entertainment centre)*
*© Richard Cooper*

There is a volume on Galician surnames by Alexander Beider which is similar to his work on Polish surnames. A copy of this book, *A Dictionary of Jewish Surnames from Galicia,* is in the JGSGB library.

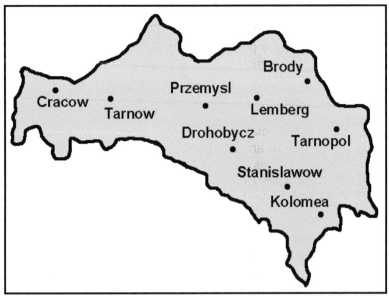
*Map of Galicia (courtesy Gesher Galicia Inc.)*

## What records are available

Civil registration began in 1784 and records were maintained by the Jewish Community, the local *Kehilla*. Most surviving records cover the years from 1850. These records are in Polish and German. There were no formal regulations or consistency in record-keeping with headings in Latin, borrowed from the Catholic Church, or German or Polish. After 1877 the format of records and data required were standardised with headings in both Polish and German.

It is worth noting that many of our Galician ancestors avoided civil marriage (though not religious marriage) and so a search of civil marriage registers may not produce information for the researcher. Any subsequent civil birth registrations might therefore show the children as illegitimate. In such cases the children may be officially known by the mother's surname rather than the father's surname.

The best and most detailed information on Galician Jewish research can be found in Suzan Wynne's two books (see Bibliography) both available in the JGSGB library. The second of these, *The Galitzianers* provides a detailed introduction to the life of the Jews of Galicia and the many political changes to the region, its boundaries and administration which had an impact on their communities. This is very useful in explaining the background and the operation of a number of regulations which can make the work of the researcher more difficult than in other parts of Poland: the adoption of surnames, the civil marriage laws and military service/conscription requirements. There are chapters on vital records (births, marriages and deaths) as well as census and notary records. There is also an overview of the holdings of some specific archive repositories such as those in the Central State Historical Archives in Lviv, now in Ukraine and in the YIVO Institute for Jewish Research in New York.

An important feature of the book is a series of appendices with reference material. There is a sample letter to a Polish archive and examples of the vital record documents that you are likely to come across. Other useful resources explained in some detail cover the use of business directories and various Holocaust-related materials including *Yizkor* (Memorial) books and the holdings of Yad Vashem.

The final appendix of some 200 pages covers the Galician towns where Jews lived in 1877 and shows the town, the main district and the sub-district. A similar section appears in Suzan Wynne's earlier book and it remains a very useful way of identifying towns where our ancestors might have lived. We are reminded that people don't always give the name of their small village once they travel far away as it is unlikely to be known by those whom they meet. Instead, they give the name of the nearest large town and this is often the reason why researchers are disappointed when they cannot find evidence of them in records of the larger town. These lists allow us to widen our field of research.

**Locating Records**

Many Galician vital records have survived and can be found at archives in Poland and Ukraine. Although no Galician-wide census has survived, there are Jewish or town census records for a few key towns. For **Polish Galicia**, vital records to about 1905 and any available census records can be found at the regional branches of the Polish State Archives.

| 1 | 2 | | | | | 3 | | | | | 4 | | | | 5 |
|---|---|---|---|---|---|---|---|---|---|---|---|---|---|---|---|
| Liczba porządkowa Fortlaufende Zahl | Urodzenia der Geburt | | | | | Obrzezania lub nadania imienia Der Beschneidung oder Namensbeilegung | | | | | Dziecięcia des Kindes | | | | Urodzenie ślubne, nieślubne ehelich oder uneheliche Geburt |
| | dzień Tag | miesiąc Monat | rok Jahr | miejsce Ort | Nr. domu Haus Nr. | dzień Tag | miesiąc Monat | rok Jahr | miejsce Ort | Nr. domu Haus Nr. | Imię Name | | płeć Geschlecht | | |
| | | | | | | | | | | | | | męska männlich | żeńska weiblich | |
| 422 | 2 | Październik Nov | 1883 | Tarnów zamieście Zabłocie | 72 | 6 | Październik Nov | 1883 | Tarnów zamieście Zabłocie | 72 | Meita | | | żeńska nieślubna | |

*(Above and overleaf) Birth record from Galicia in 'columnar' rather than 'Napoleonic' format. Column headings are in German as well as Polish*

| 6 | 7 | 8 | 9 | 10 | 11 | 12 |
|---|---|---|---|---|---|---|
| Imię i nazwisko ojca, jakość jego stan, zatrudnienie, i miejsce zamieszkania. Vor- und Zuname des Vaters, sowie Stand, Beschäftigung und Wohnort | Imię i nazwisko matki, jej stan i zamieszkanie, jakotéż imię i nazwisko, zatrudnienie i miejsce zamieszkania jej rodziców. Vor- und Zuname der Mutter, ihr Stand u. Wohnort, dann Vor- u. Zuname, Beschäftigung und Wohnort ihrer Aeltern | Własnoręczny podpis z wymienieniem zatrudnienia i miejsce zamieszkania / Eigenhändige Unterschrift mit Angabe der Beschäftigung und des Wohnortes | | | dziecię nieżywo urodzone todt geborene Kinder | Uwaga Anmerkung |
| | | kumów lub świadków, Sandeka lub Schemes der Pathen oder Zeugen, des Sandeko oder Schames | obrzezającego lub obrzezujących des oder der Beschneider | akuszerki lub akuszora der Hebamme oder des Geburtshelfers | | |

In the 1960s, the Soviet Union and Poland agreed to transfer the former Galician vital records from Lviv to Warsaw. Therefore **Ukrainian Galicia** vital records for most towns to about 1905 can be found at the Central Archive for Historical Acts (AGAD) in Warsaw. However, some vital records were not transferred and remain at the Lviv, Ukraine archive. Most of these are records from before 1877.

Any census records that exist will be found at the Lviv, Ukraine State Archive or the local *oblast* (provincial) archive. For example, the 1890 Tarnopol Jewish census can be found in Lviv and the 1810 Jewish census in the Tarnopol *oblast* archive.

There are very few Galician records that have been microfilmed by the Mormons. No microfilms of Jewish records from the Lviv archive exist. Researching in Galicia is more likely to necessitate a trip to Poland and/or the hiring of a professional researcher than for other parts of Poland.

## Tips for Galician research

- Always try to acquire records starting in 1877 as they have more genealogical information. For example, if your grandfather born in 1870 had siblings born from 1865 until 1885, to help fill out your family tree, search for the record of any sibling born after 1876.

- In Galicia, birth records have the most valuable genealogical information. Records from 1877 nearly always give the names of the mother's parents, her father's occupation and their place of residence. For the father, there is usually no reference at all to his parents, although records usually show his occupation and place of residence.

- Birth records sometimes show notes of subsequent events that affected the civil status of the subject. For example, a note may be added when someone dies giving date of death and where the person is buried.

- Marriage records are also good sources for research. Many show information on the birth, previous marriages, military service and other aspects of the life of the groom and the bride.

- Death records do not show much additional genealogical data beyond date, place and cause of death. Usually a man's death record does not identify any family members. However, a married or widowed woman's record shows the name of the husband and a child's records usually shows the father's or mother's name and sometimes both.

- The *Gesher Galicia* special interest group publishes its own magazine and Family Finder and has a web-based discussion forum. Go to **www.jewishgen.org/Galicia/**

Rzeczpospolita Polska        Województwo _Tarnopolskie_

Urząd metrykalny izraelicki w _Husiatynie_    Powiat _Kopyczyniecki_

L. _156/1930_

# Świadectwo urodzin

_Zoff, polecenie Starostwa pow Kopyczynie z 17/10 1930 L. 4000/30_

z księgi urodzin okręgu metrykalnego izr. _Husiatyn_   Tom _VI_ Stronica _274_

| | | | |
|---|---|---|---|
| 1 | Liczba porządkowa | | _193_ |
| 2 | Urodzenia | Dzień | _17 km / siedmnastego_ |
| | | Miesiąc | _December_ |
| | | Rok | _897 / osiemset dziewięćdziesiąt siedem_ |
| | | Miejsce | _Hussiatyn_ |
| | | Nr. domu | _№_ |
| 3 | Obrzeza-nia lub nadawania imienia | Dzień | _24 km_ |
| | | Miesiąc | _December_ |
| | | Rok | _897_ |
| | | Miejsce | _Hussiatyn_ |
| | | Nr. domu | _№_ |
| 4 | Dziecięcia | Imię | _Abraham_ |
| | | Płeć — męska | _mänlich_ |
| | | Płeć — żeńska | |
| 5 | Ślubne, rzekomo ślubne lub nieślubne | | _unehelich_ |
| 6 | Imię i nazwisko, stan, zatrudnienie i miejsce zamieszkania ojca | | _Froim Klinger verheiratet nach mos. Ritus. Eierpacker in Hussiatyn_ |
| 7 | Imię i nazwisko, stan, miejsce zamieszkania matki i jej rodziców | | _Jolde Reichman verheiratet nach mos. Ritus Tochter des Jacob u. der Freude Reichman aus Skalat_ |
| 8 | Własnoręczny podpis, zatrudnie-nie i miejsce zamieszkania | kumów lub świad-ków, sandeka lub szamesa | _Pinkas Horwitz_ |
| 9 | | obrzezującego lub obrzezujących | _Nuchym Friedman_ |
| 10 | | akuszera lub akuszerki | _Libe Jides Tokajer_ |
| 11 | Dzieci nieżywo urodzone | | |
| 12 | UWAGA | | _Ich bekenne mich für Vaterschaft des Kindes Froim Klinger als zeuge u. Namensfertiger Jos Ekstein_ |

Że powyższy wyciąg z dotyczącym wpisem księgi metrykalnej zupełnie się zgadza, potwierdza się niniejszem

_Kopyczynce_ dnia _24 pazdziernika_ 19_30_

Birth certificate for Abraham Klinger (born Husiatyn, Galicia, 1897).
Certificate issued in 1930 when he became naturalised in the UK.

# 8

# PRUSSIAN POLAND

Prussia, a former kingdom and independent German state, was located in north-central Europe and included present-day northern Germany and northern Poland

- **1812** Prussian Jews were emancipated, the first German state to do so. Prussian citizenship led to surname adoption in this year. There was also a Jewish census taken and some returns still exist and were microfilmed by the Mormons.

- From emancipation until 1873, Jewish vital records were recorded and maintained separately from other religious groups. During this period in Prussia, family registers and census-like arrival/departure records were kept in towns. Recording every family and its comings and goings, these are excellent records if they exist for your town.

- Prussian records were recorded in German Gothic script, which can be very difficult to read.

- **1871** Unification of the German states by Bismarck. The areas of Poland that came under Prussian control were East and West Prussia, Pomerania, Posen and Silesia.

- **1874** Germany instituted a civil registration system, where all births, marriages, divorces and deaths were recorded by one registrar. Separate registers for religious denominations ceased to exist.

Relative to other parts of Poland, fewer Jews lived in Prussian Poland so searching for your ancestors' records for the period starting in 1874 is more difficult. Only one to five percent of the records were for Jews and these were interspersed amongst those of the majority Christian population. However, these records do identify the religion of the subject.

## Locating Records

Records for Prussian Poland can be found at regional branches of the Polish State Archives as well as repositories in Berlin, Leipzig and Potsdam, Germany. Many of the pre-unification Jewish records (before 1874) have not survived. Where they do exist, the majority have been microfilmed by the Mormons, including records in repositories in both Poland and Germany. Post-unification records have not been microfilmed by the Mormons.

The German civil records starting in 1874 were in a pre-printed format that allowed for additional personal information to be added at a later date.

## Research Tips

- It is possible that you may have enough information about your Prussian family to skip the 1874 and subsequent records. If so, you can then use the earlier records which have been microfilmed by the Mormons. Go to **www.familysearch.org** and search the library catalogue.

- It may be worthwhile joining forces with others researching the same Prussian towns to hire a professional researcher. You could also form a JRI-Poland Shtetl Co-Op to work together on the Mormon films and index or extract the vital records.

- Read the Prussian section in the *Avotaynu Guide to Jewish Genealogy.*

- Get a crib sheet for German Gothic script or find someone who is able to help you decipher it.

# 9

# BIALYSTOK – RUSSIAN PALE OF SETTLEMENT

Most of the former Russian *gubernia* of Grodno is now in Belarus. A much smaller part, whose main city is Bialystok, is now in Poland. This area was under direct Russian rule from 1815 (Congress of Vienna) until the end of World War One, when Poland was reconstituted. It has been Poland since this time apart from 1939 to 1941 when it was occupied by Russia and from 1941 to 1945 when it was occupied by Nazi Germany.

Record-keeping was similar throughout the Pale of Settlement (Latvia, Lithuania, Belarus, Ukraine and Moldova.)

- **1826** Jewish vital record registration began. Events were registered in local synagogues. For the Bialystok area these have not survived.

- **1835** Local rabbis were required to register and maintain the vital record registers for the Russian crown. The registers were in columnar format in Russian and many were later copied in Hebrew. The columnar format did not change between 1835 and 1918. Unlike Galicia and similar to Congress Poland, marriage was not an issue and most Jewish marriages were registered with the civil authorities.

Unfortunately, in this area of Poland, few Jewish vital records have survived. Only the City of Bialystok and ten nearby towns have any vital records and, for most of these towns, many years are missing. Bialystok has records dating back to 1835, but even here there are many years missing between 1835 and 1875. The information in vital records in the Pale is not as extensive as that contained in records from Congress Poland or Galicia.

These vital records are held at the Polish State Archive branch in Bialystok and at some local civil records offices. JRI-Poland has indexed all available records at the Bialystok branch archives.

In the Pale of Settlement, Jews were required to adopt surnames in 1809. This was to enable the government to tax Jews and conscript their sons into the army, sometimes at the age of 14 and for up to 25 years. Jews therefore avoided this registration if possible and many did not adopt family names until about 1830.

The Russian Empire mandated a series of revision lists (*reviski skazki*) which are similar to the books of residents in Congress Poland. The objective was again to develop tax rolls and conscription lists. This census started in 1795, at about the time that the Russian Empire acquired a large Jewish population through the partitions of Poland. These lists would be updated over time until the next list was created. There were ten lists from 1795 to 1858 and the 1858 list was updated until the end of the 19th century.

---

**Information in 1858 Russian Empire revision lists**

- **Town / Uyezd / Gubernia**
- **Family Surname**
- **Given Name**
- **Father's Given Name**
- **Relationship to Head of Household**
- **Present Age / Age at Last Revision**
- **Reason Left [e.g. moved, conscripted, died]**
- **Year left**
- **Page Number**
- **Date**
- **Family Registration Number**
- **Type of Record**

---

For those with ancestors in this area, these lists could be a valuable source of genealogical information. Based on information from the Belarus SIG, it is thought that the Belarus Historical Archive in Grodno has the revision lists and updates for Bialystok, Bielsk and Sokoloka *Uyezd* (counties) from 1816 to about 1885. Unfortunately, access to these archives has proved difficult. In 2003, a Bialystok region Jewish genealogy group, Bialygen, was formed to combine resources to gain access to these revision lists. Information on this group and its work can be found at
**www.shtetlinks.jewishgen.org/BialyGen/Homepage.htm**

# 10
# READING POLISH RECORDS

The excitement of acquiring records from various sources is often tempered by the realisation that extracting information from them is going to be difficult. Some of the problems are those which affect old documents from any country - difficult handwriting, ink blots obscuring key words, deterioration of the document over time, faint copies. Other issues relate to documents in foreign languages and/or scripts, the administrative 'legalese' in which they may be written and grammatical forms of the language which can confuse you.

Most Polish birth, marriage and death records from the first half of the 19th century are handwritten in Polish and are in a continuous, narrative style known as the Napoleonic format. They are not in a form or in columns (though the latter are found in Galicia.) Dates and ages are all written out in words instead of numbers. After 1868 the records are written in Cyrillic (Russian) script.

Many of these problems can be overcome by using some of the excellent handbooks and leaflets available. However, it must be emphasised that time and patience will be needed. Researchers will have to learn and practice the techniques - it does get easier over time and it means that you do not always have to rely on the goodwill or expertise of someone who speaks the language.

A few tips to make life easier:

- Get a sheet of clear yellow acetate to lay over faded records. This darkens the ink and can make some parts clearer.

- Work from a photocopy to avoid damaging the original.

- Underline or use a yellow highlighter on the photocopy to pick out names and other important information.

- It is not necessary to translate an entire record to be able to extract the important information.

- Have a Russian alphabet crib-sheet to hand showing both printed and handwritten characters. (See Chapter 14.)

- As a minimum, find a list of numbers, days and months in the document language so that you can work out dates and ages. If you know the number for "three", the chances are that you will recognise similar words that might be "thirteen" or "thirty": common sense should tell you that a person's age at marriage is unlikely to be three or thirteen but that it might be thirty. (See Chapter 13.)

**Birth records** usually give the name, age and occupation of the father, found near the beginning of the document. The mother's name, often including her maiden name, is usually found a couple of lines before the child's name, which comes towards the end. Other people named in the document are witnesses, whose ages and occupations may be given. The key information tends to appear in the same place in each record so, after a while, you can start to extract the relevant information more quickly.

**Marriage records** are longer documents and usually give details about the parents of the bride and groom. It is important to note if the bride or groom came from another town. This will save you work and frustration if you have tried, unsuccessfully, to find evidence of this family in the same town at an earlier date.

**Death records** can sometimes be very helpful if they have a list of the surviving family of the deceased - the spouse and/or children. A list of the latter is often, though not always, in chronological order of birth and allows you to check if a child has predeceased a parent.

Samples of all these certificate types can be found at
**www.JewishGen.org/jri-pl/frazin.htm**

One of the most accessible and useful books for extracting this information is Judith Frazin's *A Translation Guide to 19th-Century Polish-Language Civil-Registration Documents.* This provides examples of documents and a method for identifying key words and sections so that you can locate the relevant information. It has word and vocabulary lists divided into sections such as occupation, family and marriage. There is a list of personal names and an indication of whether they were male or female. A Russian alphabet is also included as is a sheet with numbers, dates and key vocabulary.

Other useful books include Jonathan Shea and William Hoffman's series *In Their Own Words - A Genealogist's Translation Guide to Polish, German, Latin and Russian Documents.* Volume 1 covers Polish documents; volume 2 Russian documents. These go beyond birth, marriage and death records and include census, probate, passport and other documents. There are examples of all the documents, explanations, translations and word lists. The books also contain maps and sample letters to archives as well as information on the structure of the language and how this may affect what you see in the written document.
See also **www.langline.com/StateArchGuide.htm**

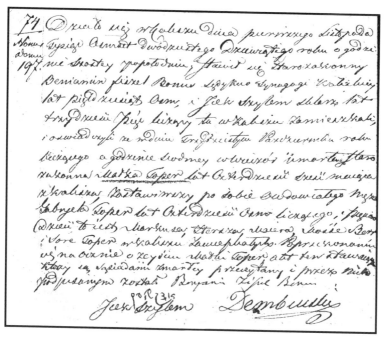

*Death record from Kalisz for Malka Toper (1829). The record also lists her husband (Gabryel) and children Markus, Hersz, Maier, Moise Ber and Sore*

# 11
# NAMES AND GRAMMATICAL VARIATIONS

Names in Polish records may have varied spellings according to whether they are being used for men or women and on their position in a sentence. You need to be aware of this and understand what the basic name form might be.

- Surnames ending in *–cki* or *–ski* are used only for males; the female version ends in *–cka* or *–ska* eg *Kaliski/Kaliska*. Bear in mind that if the family emigrated from Poland, particularly to an English-speaking country, they might have chosen one version, probably the father's, for use on documentation in their new country, to ensure consistency.

- In English we say "We're having dinner at the Robinsons'." In this sentence, Robinsons' means at the house of the Robinson family. You need to remove the grammatical ending (here, the s'), in order to get the basic surname, "Robinson". In Polish you need to remove/transform the grammatical ending in a similar way. Forms such as *Goldbergów, Sawickich, Kowalskich* are the grammatical forms of the surnames *Goldberg, Sawicki and Kowalski*.

- In many records, the maiden name of a married woman is given in the form such as *z Goldbergów*, literally meaning "of the Goldbergs". If a surname ends in *-cka* or *-ska* then the plural is *-ich*, so *Sawicka* becomes *z Sawickich*, *Kowalska* becomes *z Kowalskich*.

- Some maiden names are actually *patronymics* based on the father's given name (ie his first name) For example, *z Berków* means "of the family of Berek", ie. daughter of Berek.

Other grammatical endings used with names include:

- *-owicz* = son of

- *-ówna* = daughter of (*-ównej*, in some grammatical forms)

- *-owa* = wife of (*-owe'*, in some grammatical forms)

In Napoleonic format birth registrations, the mother's forename will most often also be in the possessive form. For example, in a birth registration the mother's name might appear as *Chai Gitli*, but her name is actually *Chaia Gitla*. The Polish text in the registration says that the child was born *z małżonki jego Chai Gitli*, meaning "of his wife Chaia Gitla".

Here are some examples of the conversion of a name back to its basic (nominative) form:

- *Ryfki* → *Ryfka*

- *Szeyny* → *Szeyna*

- *Laj* → *Laja*

- *Hai* → *Haia*

---

**For grammar junkies (others can skip this section)**

Polish is a western Slavonic language and is one of the most difficult to learn. It retains features, such as nasal vowels (ą and ę), which have disappeared from most other Slavonic languages and something called 'palatalisation' where hard consonants such as b, g, and d change to change to p, k and t after certain vowels.

Nouns are masculine, feminine or neuter and are declined (change their endings) depending on their position in the sentence. The endings of adjectives have to agree with the nouns they describe.

---

# 12
# POLISH PRONUNCIATION

Unless you are planning a visit to Poland, you won't need to say anything in the language. However, it helps to understand the pronunciation of certain letters when you are trying to work out the names of towns and people.

| Letters | English equivalent pronunciation |
|---|---|
| aj | i as in sight |
| au | ow as in cow |
| ą | on in the middle of a word; more nasal, as in the French garçon when at the end of a word |
| c | ts as in mats |
| ch | ch as in the Scottish loch |
| ci/cz/ć | ch as in churn |
| dz | ds as in goods; or dj, similar to the j in Japan; ts as in mats when at the end of a word |
| dzi/dź/dż | dj, similar to the j in Japan; ch as in churn when at the end of a word |
| ej | ay as in pay |
| ę | en as in endorse in the middle of a word; e as in set when at the end of a word; em as in hem if followed by b or p |
| h | ch as in the Scottish loch |
| i | ee as in need; sometimes I as in sit |
| j | y as in yes |
| ł | w as in water |
| ni/ń | a slight n-y sound as in nuance |
| ó | oo as in look |

| | |
|---|---|
| rz | s as in trea**s**ure; sh as in **sh**ot when at the end of a word |
| si/sz/ś | sh as in **sh**ot |
| u | oo as in l**oo**k |
| w | v as in **v**oice |
| y | i as in r**i**ch |
| zi/ź/ż | s as in trea**s**ure; sh as in **sh**ot when at the end of a word |

The Polish consonants, **b, d, g, w** and **z** are generally pronounced like the English b, d, g, v and z but at the end of a word or when coming before certain letters, the pronunciation softens to become p, t, k, f and s respectively.

In Polish, the stress is always on the last but one syllable of the word.

When **e (or ę)** occurs at the end of a Polish word, it is always pronounced eg **inne** (another) is pronounced 'een-neh'

If you are looking for words in a Polish dictionary, it helps to know the order of the alphabet. Some letters may look like English letters but they have a separate place in the alphabet.

a, ą, b, c, ć, d, e, ę, f, g, h, i, j, k, l, ł, m, n, ń, o, ó, p, q, r, s, ś, t, u, w, x, y, z, ź, ż

*The order of the Polish alphabet*

qwertzuiopżś
asdfghjklłąó
yxcvbnm

*Layout of the Polish keyboard*

# 13
# WORD LIST FOR POLISH DATES AND NUMBERS

## Numbers

In many genealogical records, numbers are spelled out. The following list gives the cardinal (1, 2, 3) and ordinal (1st, 2nd, 3rd) numbers. Dates are written in ordinal form. In dates, ordinal numbers usually end with *-ego*, for example:

| | |
|---|---|
| *pierwszy* | the first |
| *pierwszego* | on the first (of the month) |

| **Cardinal** | | **Ordinal** | |
|---|---|---|---|
| 1 | *jeden, jedna* | 1st | *pierwszy* |
| 2 | *dwa* | 2nd | *drugi* |
| 3 | *trzy* | 3rd | *trzeci* |
| 4 | *cztery* | 4th | *czwarty* |
| 5 | *pięć* | 5th | *piąty* |
| 6 | *sześć* | 6th | *szósty* |
| 7 | *siedem* | 7th | *siódmy* |
| 8 | *osiem* | 8th | *ósmy* |
| 9 | *dziewęć* | 9th | *dziewiąty* |
| 10 | *dziesięć* | 10th | *dziesiąty* |
| 11 | *jedenaście* | 11th | *jedenasty* |
| 12 | *dwanaście* | 12th | *dwunasty* |
| 13 | *trzynaście* | 13th | *trzynasty* |
| 14 | *czternaście* | 14th | *czternasty* |
| 15 | *piętnaście* | 15th | *piętnasty* |
| 16 | *szesnaście* | 16th | *szesnasty* |
| 17 | *siedemnaście* | 17th | *siedemnasty* |

| | | | | |
|---|---|---|---|---|
| 18 | osiemnaście | 18th | osiemnasty |
| 19 | dziewiętnaście | 19th | dziewiętnasty |
| 20 | dwadzieścia | 20th | dwudziesty, dwódziesty |
| 21 | dwadzieścia jeden | 21st | dwudziesty pierwszy |
| 22 | dwadzieścia dwa | 22nd | dwudziesty drugi |
| 30 | trzydzieści | 30th | trzydziesty |
| 40 | czterdzieści | 40th | czterdziesty |
| 50 | pięćdzieśiąt | 50th | pięćdziesiąty |
| 60 | sześćdzieśiąt | 60th | sześćdziesiąty |
| 70 | siedemdzieśiąt | 70th | siedemdziesiąty |
| 80 | osiemdziesiąt | 80th | osiemdziesiąty |
| 90 | dziewięćdiesiąt | 90th | dziewięćdziesiśty |
| 100 | sto | 100th | setny |
| 200 | dwieście | 200th | dwóchsetny |
| 300 | trzysta | 300th | trzysetny, trzechsetny |
| 400 | czterysta | 400th | czterysetny, czterechsetny |
| 500 | pięćset | 500th | pięćsetny |
| 600 | sześćset | 600th | szęćsetny |
| 700 | siedemset | 700th | siedemsetny |
| 800 | osiemset | 800th | osiemsetny |
| 900 | dziewięćset | 900th | dziewięćsetny |
| 1000 | tysiąc | 1000th | tysięczny |

## Dates and time

In Polish records, dates are usually written out, for example:
*roku tysiąc osemset trzydziestego szóstego dnia dwódziestego trzeciego marca* translates as : in the year one thousand eight hundredth thirtieth and sixth on the day twentieth third of March (23 March 1836)

In some records, two dates are recorded:
*dnia piątego/siedemnastego Maja* on the day 5th/17th of May. The two dates are usually 12 days apart. The first date is based on the Julian calendar, used by the Russian Empire; the second is based on the present-day Gregorian calendar.

## Months

| English | Polish* |
|---------|---------|
| January | *stycznia* |
| February | *lutego* |
| March | *marca* |
| April | *kwietnia* |
| May | *maja* |
| June | *czerwca* |
| July | *lipca* |
| August | *sierpnia* |
| September | *wrzesnia* |
| October | *października* |
| November | *listopada* |
| December | *grudnia* |

*This is how the month is written in documents. A dictionary will show you another form.

## Days of the week

| English | Polish |
|---------|--------|
| Sunday | *niedziela* |
| Monday | *poniedziałek* |
| Tuesday | *wtorek* |
| Wednesday | *środa* |
| Thursday | *czwartek* |
| Friday | *piątek* |
| Saturday | *sobota* |

## Times of the day

Polish birth and death records often indicate the exact time of day when the birth or death occurred. This is usually written out.

| Polish | English |
|---|---|
| *o godzinie drugiej* | at the second hour |
| *o godzinie siódmej* | at the seventh hour |
| *w nocy* | at night |
| *południe/w południe* | noon |
| *popołudniu/z południa* | afternoon |
| *przed południem* | forenoon |
| *północna godzina* | midnight |
| *rano/z rana* | in the morning |
| *wieczorem/w wieczór* | in the evening |

*Unknown Warsaw couple (courtesy J. Samson)*

# CYRILLIC/ RUSSIAN ALPHABET

| Printed letters | Handwritten letters | English equivalent pronunciation |
|---|---|---|
| А а | *Аа* | a as in b**a**d |
| Б б | *Бб* | b |
| В в | *Вв* | v |
| Г г | *Гг* | g as in **g**ap |
| Д д | *Дд* | d |
| Е е | *Ее* | ye as in **ye**s |
| ё | *ё* | yo as in **yo**nder |
| Ж ж | *Жж* | s as in trea**s**ure |
| З з | *Зз* | z as in **z**ebra |
| И и | *Ии* | ee as in b**ee** |
| й | *й* | ee as in b**ee** |
| К к | *Кк* | k |
| Л л | *Лл* | l |
| М м | *Мм* | m |
| Н н | *Нн* | n |
| О о | *Оо* | o as in **o**r |
| П п | *Пп* | p |
| Р р | *Рр* | r |

| | | |
|---|---|---|
| С с | *C c* | s |
| Т т | *Тт m* | t |
| У у | *У у* | oo as in b**oo**t |
| Ф ф | *Ф ф* | f |
| Х х | *Х х* | ch as in lo**ch** |
| Ц ц | *Ц ц* | ts as in ra**ts** |
| Ч ч | *Ч ч* | ch as in **ch**eese |
| Ш ш | *Ш ш* | sh as in **sh**ut |
| Щ щ | *Щ щ* | shch as in fre**sh ch**eese |
| ы | *ы* | i as in wr**i**t |
| ъ | *ъ* | hard sign (not pronounced) |
| ь | *ь* | soft sign (not pronounced) |
| Э э | *Э э* | e as in b**e**g |
| Ю ю | *Ю ю* | u as in **u**se |
| Я я | *Я я* | ya as in **ya**rd |

In 1918, the alphabet was modified and some letters were changed or removed, such as ѣ which appeared at the end of words ending with certain letters. It had no sound itself. Similarly, in the alphabet above, the hard and soft signs appear after certain letters but are not pronounced.

йцукенгшщзхъ
фывапролджэ
ячсмитьбю.

*Layout of the Russian keyboard*

# 15
## PLANNING A VISIT TO POLAND

Once you have done as much documentary research as possible into your family in your own country and used online resources, you might want to visit the towns or villages where your ancestors came from. In a way, this is an attempt to complete the picture of their lives – to visit places they used to go to, such as a school or a synagogue, and to get a feel of what their life might have been like. But don't get too carried way with what you might find – Poland as we know it today didn't exist in the 19th century! It was partitioned amongst Austria, Russia and Prussia. This means that the vital documents concerning your ancestors might be in German, Russian or Polish. In addition some towns, which were once in Poland, today might be in Germany or Ukraine. So if you decide to go there, be prepared to find nothing. Then if you are lucky enough to get some positive results, you should be delighted.

Undertaking a research trip to Eastern Europe requires patience, planning and an understanding that comfort levels in hotels in some places are unlikely to be the same as you might expect in your own country or when travelling to a popular holiday destination.

Try to avoid visiting Poland in the depths of winter when it may be cold with snow hampering your travel arrangements. On the other hand, do not think of Eastern Europe as a place of eternal Siberian chill. In the summer it can get extremely hot.

If you have an address where your family lived, the building may no longer be standing or may now be used for other purposes. Many towns still have cemeteries, but again, don't be too upset if there are no gravestones or only ones which have been vandalised or damaged by the weather. It is unlikely (though not impossible) that anyone will have taken it upon themselves to care for a disused cemetery after all these years and if you do find one, it may be overgrown. Cemeteries are listed in Miriam Weiner's book *Jewish Roots in Poland* (Routes to Roots Foundation), a copy of which is in JGSGB's library.

## Before your trip

Use the resources mentioned in this Guide to get as much information as you can on family names and any associated locations. What you should be looking for on your trip is material that is difficult to access in any other way - archives that have not been microfilmed or indexed. Make a list of your research goals but accept that you may need to modify it as you go along. There may be unexpected finds but it probably helps in your initial and subsequent contacts with the archives to be as specific as possible.

*Leżajsk Jewish Cemetery © Richard Cooper*

If you know where your ancestors lived, you will obviously want to go to those towns. Contact the archive about your impending visit several weeks before you leave home. Miriam Weiner's book gives the addresses of branches of the Polish State Archives (PSA) which hold birth, marriage and death certificates for every town in today's Poland. You can then write to the archive. If the PSA website shows an email address or phone number for the local archive, you may prefer to contact them by these means. You need to find out the opening hours and whether anyone there speaks English.

Do not expect to find the scenario frequently shown in the British television series *Who do you think you are?* where the welcoming archivist, clutching a sheaf of relevant family documents, rushes out to meet the visitor. You are more likely to find an old building which has not seen a coat of paint for years and which contains large, dusty volumes of handwritten records.

## Checklist

- Go on to **www.JewishGen.org/jgff** and type in the town you want to visit. There you will find names of other genealogists who have an interest in the same town and may have visited it. Email some of them, perhaps the latest on the page, to ask for up-to-date information. This website also offers you the opportunity to put in name of families in which you are interested. Previous postings to JewishGen, JGSGB-Discuss or articles in journals such as *Shemot* could also be searched for such information.

- If you are visiting **Warsaw,** plan to visit the **Jewish Historical Institute** which contains a wealth of information on Polish Jewry. It contains a museum, a library, old maps, trade and phone directories and much more. Exhibitions are frequently held there showing the Ghetto and old photos of Warsaw and its Jews.
  To make an appointment contact:

    Żydowski Instytut Historyczny
    00-090 Warszawa
    ul. Tlomackie 3/5
    Tel: 00 (22) 827 92 21
    Fax: 00 (22) 827 83 72
    Email: **secretary@jhi.pl**

Various joint indexing projects are being undertaken between JRI-Poland and the Jewish Historical Institute. These include:

- Kraków Marriage and Banns Registers, 1877 - 1939
- Wrocław *Matzevah*/gravestone files, ca 1900 - 1939
- Biala Podlaska, Jewish census, 1939
- Warsaw Cemetery records and photographs
- Polish *Aliyah*  (immigration of Jews to Israel) passports
- Warsaw Ghetto death cards

For full details of these and other projects see:
**www.jewishgen.org/jri-pl/jri-jhi.htm**

- Find out the opening hours of any archives you propose visiting.

- Make appointments with local people as many weeks in advance as you can. Meeting the local mayor may yield positive results as often more recent archives may be kept in the town hall.

## On your own or with a group?

If you are on a non-genealogical group tourist trip visiting one or several towns, you may decide to prolong your visit, staying on in the town where you already are or travelling to the one that interests you. You would have to check with the travel company whether you could extend your stay.

Alternatively, you may decide to visit Poland independently, purely for genealogical research. In this case, you must choose whether you will need a car (plus driver) and a researcher/interpreter. Your decisions will depend on your health (walking ability), your pocket (can you afford these people?), your linguistic ability (do you already know some German or Polish?) and your spirit of adventure (have you been to Eastern Europe before?). Try to stay in Poland for as long as you can – there may be problems with the best-planned trips and one or two days are unlikely to be enough if you want to do any in-depth research.

One way of combining both the group and the genealogical experience is by contacting ShtetlSchleppers. They organise group visits to various hub cities in Eastern Europe. Details can be found at: **www.JewishGen.org/ShtetlSchleppers/** The Shoreshim website also offers genealogical archive services and planned trips. **www.shoreshim.org/sho_services.asp**

Before signing up with these or any other companies you find advertised on the Internet or elsewhere, try to check out the experiences of others who have used them. Make sure that what they offer is tailored to your personal requirements and budget.

*Rzeszów , Old Synagogue (now Rzeszów Municipal Archives)*
*© Richard Cooper*

## Travelling to Poland

As well as flights with international airlines to major towns in Poland, primarily Warsaw and Kraków, it is worth investigating the budget airlines which fly from the UK to other, often smaller destinations. At the time of writing these include: Bydgoszcz, Gdańsk, Katowice, Koszalin, Łódź, Poznań, Rzeszów, Szczecin, Wrocław and Zielona Góra

Taking your own car involves a lot of driving: you would have to take a ferry to Hamburg, Rotterdam or Denmark. If you chose the latter, you would then have to take another ferry from Denmark to Świnoujście in the west of Poland. But if you are prepared to spend a week or so driving round, you could have an interesting trip. Country roads still carry horses and carts and night driving should be undertaken with care.

To travel by train to Poland, take Eurostar to Brussels and a high-speed train to Cologne, then a direct sleeper train to Warsaw. Alternatively take Eurostar to Brussels, the sleeper train to Berlin, then an express to Warsaw, Kraków, Poznań, Wrocław or Katowice. Information can be found at
**www.seat61.com/Poland.htm**

## Travelling around Poland

Hiring a self-drive car is quite expensive but you may be less likely to be spotted as a foreigner. A better option is to hire a car with an English-speaking driver. This has the advantage that, hopefully, your driver will know the route, will be able to ask in Polish if he loses his way, and at your destination might be able to ask local people for any particular place you wish to find.

Within Poland, there is a fairly comprehensive rail network and fares are comparatively cheap by British standards. Most towns have a railway station and if you are based in one town and making trips to other places, it is a good idea to visit the station a day or two before your journey to check out train times and perhaps buy your ticket in advance. To reach smaller places, you might need a bus. Enquire at the local tourist office for help and information.

## How to find a researcher/interpreter/guide

If you need one, this is probably one of the most important aspects of your planning. The best course of action is to post a message on the JewishGen discussion group

**www.JewishGen.org/JewishGen/DiscussionGroup.htm**

Ask for the experiences of those who have already visited the area and used researchers/interpreters. They will give you an idea of costs and contact details. Personal recommendations are important - you need a guide/interpreter who will understand your genealogical needs and be able to help you negotiate with officials and archives. The local tourist office in your chosen town may also be able to help.

## Dealing with officials

Once you are in Poland, you should be aware that ways of thinking and working in Eastern Europe have only recently begun to change and concepts of customer service are only slowly taking root. As with archives everywhere, resources, staffing and funding may be limited and the ability to handle direct queries from researchers may be a problem. Again, finding out the experiences of those who have already visited Poland is probably the best way to proceed.

## In the archives

Having found out the opening hours before leaving home, ensure that you make maximum use of your limited time in the archive. Some offices close for lunch and if the building is outside the town, you might want to take refreshments with you, as there may not be a café. It is advisable always to take your passport with you.

If you hire a private researcher to visit the archive on your behalf, it may be necessary to provide a letter of 'Limited Power of Attorney', authorising them to obtain records for you. The letter should include details on how you are related to the person whose record you are requesting. Similarly, if you are hoping to carry out research for someone else, you will also need such a document which you should obtain before you leave home. Advice on how to prepare these should be sought from a solicitor or from your local Citizens'

Advice Bureau. Fellow genealogists with prior experience of visiting Polish archives may have examples that you could use or adapt.

Once you have told the officials what documents you want, you may have to fill in forms and then have to wait until the relevant record books arrive. To find birth, marriage or death certificates, you will have to go through registers, probably one for each year. Each entry will have been made at the time, so is in date order, with a record number (*akt*) beside it. At the end of each register there is usually an alphabetical list of names, with either the *akt* number and/or the record book page number. You can search more quickly if you find these lists first, and then go to the record/page corresponding to these numbers. The indexes are usually ordered alphabetically by surname but some may be listed by first name.

*Part of an 1858 death index in alphabetical order of first name rather than surname. The left column shows the record (Akt) numbers.*

The certificates will have been handwritten in Polish, Russian or German, depending on the locality and can be difficult to read. Take some slips of paper with you to insert at each page where you will want to take a photocopy.

Some local civil registration offices (USC) or branches of the Polish State Archives (PSA) charge for a certified copy of an extract; others may give you an unstamped, unofficial extract for nothing, as a favour. As with all archives, the availability of photocopies will depend on a number of factors: the age, size and condition of the record book, the rules for copying at that archive and the operating state of the photocopier.

*Dąbrowa Tarnowska, synagogue*
*© Richard Cooper*

### Reading documents

See Chapter 10 (Reading Polish records) in this Guide. One problem is where the dates are written in words, so you cannot quickly scan each document by eye to check if it is the right one. You will probably save time in the long run by photocopying all documents which you think pertain to your family. You don't want to return home and realize that you should have copied more documents. It is also probably cheaper to do this while on site. You might find it useful to take a dictionary with you and the Polish word list which you can often buy at LDS Family History Centres or download from the FamilySearch website at **www.familysearch.org**

If you know the streets where your ancestors lived, you might want to check to see if other documents, such as censuses or land registry lists, are available. The holdings of different archives will vary, so again the value of preparation before your trip cannot be overemphasised.

## Recording your trip

You may find it useful to buy a small 'trip diary' before you go and put in it the following information:

- details of your travel arrangements
- addresses of hotels and reservation information
- names and addresses of local people
- historical family addresses gleaned from your research
- addresses and phone numbers of local archives plus details of opening times
- list of relevant websites
- brief outline of your family history and names
- list of your research 'goals'

This diary can then be used to record other activities and information as you go along. It will help to remind you what you have done on your trip, whom you met, what was successful, how much things cost and also what didn't work. It will also help you document your photographs and any other materials when you come to sort these out afterwards. It could be a useful resource for planning future trips (whether for you or when contacted by other researchers) and a good basis for writing articles for publication and/or making presentations to genealogical groups.

# GLOSSARY

| | |
|---|---|
| AGAD | *Archiwum Główne Akt Dawnych*, the Main Archives of Historical Records, in Warsaw. |
| *Akt* | Polish word meaning 'document'. Often seen as a column heading in vital record indices and extracts, to denote the record numbers. (plural: *akta*). |
| banns | documents of intent to marry. (In Polish: *zapowiedzi*). |
| BMD | **B**irth, **M**arriage and **D**eath records. |
| Congress Poland | Another term for the Kingdom of Poland |
| Cyrillic | Alphabet used for the Russian language. |
| FHC | LDS (Mormon) **F**amily **H**istory **C**entre, branch library. |
| FHL | LDS (Mormon) **F**amily **H**istory **L**ibrary, in Salt Lake City, Utah. |
| Galicia | Province of Austro-Hungarian Empire 1772 until 1917. Belonged to Poland between the two world wars. Today divided between South-eastern Poland and W Ukraine. |
| *gmina* | Subdivision of a *powiat*, an administrative unit that may be one town or a group of towns and villages. Akin to a "township". |
| *gubernia* | Geographical/political subdivision of the Russian Empire, similar to a province, which applied to the Kingdom of Poland from 1844 until World War I. (Russian: Губерния). |
| JRI-Poland | Jewish Records Indexing - Poland, a database project. Website: www.JewishGen.org/jri-pl |
| *kehilla* | Local Jewish community organisation often responsible for liaison with the civil authorities. |
| Kingdom of Poland | Also known as Congress Poland or Russian Poland. It was the part of Poland occupied by the Russian Empire 1815-1918. Today this area is in east-central Poland except northern Suwałki which is in SW Lithuania. |

| | |
|---|---|
| *landsman* | Someone who originated in the same village prior to immigration (plural: **landsleit**). |
| LDS | Church of Jesus Christ of **L**atter-**d**ay **S**aints, commonly used to denote the Mormon Family History Library. |
| matronymic | Name based on the mother's given/first name. |
| *oblast* | Province |
| *obwód* | District, subdivision of a *gubernia.* |
| palatinate | Geographical/political subdivision of pre-partition Poland (before 1795), similar to a province. |
| Pale of Settlement | The 15 *gubernias* on the western edge of the Russian Empire, to which Jewish residence was restricted 1794 to 1917 |
| patronymic | Name based upon the father's given/first name. |
| *powiat* | District, subdivision of a *gubernia.* (plural: **powiaty**). |
| PSA | **P**olish **S**tate **A**rchives. |
| Russian Poland | See Kingdom of Poland |
| *starosta* | A government official, the head of a *powiat.* (plural: **starosci**). |
| *uezd/uyezd* | District, subdivision of a *gubernia.* |
| USC | *Urząd Stanu Cywilnego* - Civil Records Office where vital records less than 100 years old are usually stored in each town. |
| vital records | Birth, marriage and death records |
| *województwo* | Geographical/political subdivision of the Kingdom of Poland until its inclusion in Russia's *gubernia* system in 1844, and again following World War 1. Sometimes called a "voivod(e)ship" in English. |

# BIBLIOGRAPHY

**Beider, Alexander**
*A Dictionary of Jewish Surnames from the Kingdom of Poland*
Avotaynu Inc. (1996) ISBN 0962637394

**Beider, Alexander**
*A Dictionary of Jewish Surnames from Galicia*
Avotaynu Inc. (2004) ISBN 9781886223196

**Fox, Cyril and Issroff, Saul**
*Jewish Memorial (Yizkor) Books in the United Kingdom - Destroyed European Jewish Communities*
JGSGB (2006) ISBN 0953766950

**Frazin, Judith**
*A Translation Guide to 19th-Century Polish-Language Civil-Registration Documents*
Jewish Genealogical Society of Illinois (1989) ISBN 0961351217

**Kagan, Joram**
*Poland's Jewish Landmarks, A Travel Guide*
Hippocrene Books Inc (2001) ISBN 0781808510

**Kay, George K**
*Postal Place Names in Poland*
G K Kay (1993) ISBN 978-0951999400

**Kershaw, Roger & Mark Pearsall**
*Immigrants and Aliens: A Guide to Sources on UK Immigration and Citizenship*
The National Archives Readers Guide No. 22 Kew (2000)
ISBN 1873162944

**Laszuk, Anna**
*Księgi metrykalne i stanu cywilnego w archiwach państwowych w Polsce* (Metrical and civil registration documents in the State Archives in Poland) Warsaw: Naczelna Dyrekcja Archiwów Państwowych (Head Office of the State Archives), (1998, 2000) ISBN 8386643536.

**Mokotoff, Gary and Sack, Sallyann with Alexander Sharon**
*Where Once We Walked: A Guide to the Jewish Communities Destroyed in the Holocaust*
 Avotaynu Inc (Revised 2002) ISBN 1886223157

**Mokotoff, Gary and Sack, Sallyann (editors)**
*Avotaynu Guide to Jewish Genealogy*
Avotaynu Inc (July 2004) ISBN 9781886223165

**Shea, Jonathan D and Hoffman, William F**
*Following the Paper Trail: A Multilingual Translation Guide*
Avotaynu Inc (1994) ISBN 0962637343

**Shea, Jonathan D and Hoffman, William F**
*In Their Words: A Genealogist's Translation Guide*
*Volume 1: Polish (2000)*
Language & Lineage Press ISBN 0963157930
*Volume II: Russian (2002)*
 Language & Lineage Press ISBN 0963157949

**Weiner, Miriam**
*Jewish Roots in Poland: Pages from the Past and Archival Inventories.*
The Miriam Weiner Routes to Roots Foundation and YIVO Institute for Jewish Research, (1997) ISBN 0965650804

**Wynne, Suzan**
*Finding Your Jewish Roots in Galicia - A Resource Guide*
Avotaynu Inc. (1998) ISBN 1886223084

**Wynne, Suzan**
*The Galitzianers - The Jews of Galicia 1772-1918*
Wheatmark (2006) ISBN 1587366096

Copies of most of these books are in the JGSGB library.

# USEFUL WEBSITES

| | |
|---|---|
| Archive database (Roots to Routes Foundation) | www.rtrfoundation.org/archdta.html |
| Association of Polish Jews in Israel | www.zchor.org/hitachdut.htm |
| Avotaynu | www.avotaynu.com/ |
| Dan's Genealogy Page – Polish Links | www1.ics.uci.edu/~dan/genealogy/ |
| Dictionary (pictures) multi-language | www.ibiblio.org/yiddish/Vort/ |
| Ellis Island (Stephen Morse's shortcut) | www.JewishGen.org/databases/eidb/ellis.html |
| Exemption from internment certificates (UK) | www.movinghere.org.uk/browse/f.htm |
| Family Finder | www.JewishGen.org/jgff/ |
| FamilySearch (LDS/Mormon website) | www.familysearch.org |
| Galicia & Bukovina – a research handbook | www.ourroots.ca/e/toc.aspx?id=1563 |
| Galicia Jewish Museum | www.galiciajewishmuseum.org/en/index.html |
| German-Polish and Polish-German location names in Poland and Russia | www.atsnotes.com/other/gerpol.html |
| Jewish Records Indexing-Poland Project | www.JewishGen.org/jri-pl/ |
| JewishGen | www.JewishGen.org |
| Jews in Poland | http://cyberroad.com/poland/jews.html |
| LDS Polish film list | www.jewishgen.org/jri-pl/jri-lds.htm |
| Map of modern Poland | http://mapa.szukacz.pl/ |
| Maps of Poland | www.zum.de/whkmla/histatlas/eceurope/haxpoland.html |
| Museum of the Jewish People (*Beth Hatefutsoth*) | www.bh.org.il/index.html |

| | |
|---|---|
| Online historical directories | www.kalter.org/search.php |
| Poland information files | www.jewishgen.org/InfoFiles/#Poland |
| PolandGenWeb | www.rootsweb.com/~polwgw/ Research.html |
| Polish archive holdings of Jewish vital records | www.jewishgen.org/InfoFiles/Poland/ PolishTownsArchives.htm |
| Polish genealogical websites (Cyndi's list) | www.cyndislist.com/poland.htm |
| Polish Jewish cemeteries | www.kirkuty.xip.pl/indexang.htm |
| Polish Jews | http://polishjews.org/home.htm |
| Polish letter writing guides | www.pgsa.org/PolishLetterWriting.htm www.polishroots.org/genpoland/certif.htm |
| Polish letter-writing guide and Polish word list | www.familysearch.org (in the section on 'Getting Started' click on 'guides' ) These are also available at the JGSGB library and through LDS Family History Centres |
| Polish Roots | www.polishroots.com/ |
| Polish State Archives | www.archiwa.gov.pl/?CIDA=177 |
| Reading letters from archives | www.langline.com/StateArchGuide.htm |
| Routes to Roots | www.routestoroots.com/ |
| SEZAM archive database | http://baza.archiwa.gov.pl/sezam/pradziad. eng.php |
| ShtetlSeeker | www.JewishGen.org/ShtetlSeeker/ |
| Vital record certificate examples | www.jewishgen.org/jri-pl/frazin.htm |
| Yad Vashem | www.yadvashem.org.il/ |
| YIVO photo archive | http://yivo1000towns.cjh.org/main.asp |
| Yizkor (memorial) books | www.jewishgen.org/Yizkor/ |
| Żydów w Polsce (Jews in Poland) | www.izrael.badacz.org/zydzi_w_polsce/ katalog.html |

# INDEX

# PUBLICATIONS
# IN THE 'JEWISH ANCESTORS' SERIES

*Jewish Ancestors?*

## A Guide to Jewish Genealogy in Germany and Austria

ISBN: 0-9537669-1-8/ISBN: 978-0-9537669-1-8

**Thea Skyte and Randol Schoenberg**

**Series Editor: Rosemary Wenzerul**

◆ An insight into researching your German or Austrian family roots◆
◆An informative guide to the archives of available records◆
◆Explains how to obtain the records you thought no longer existed◆

**Price: £2.00 + 50p p&p (US$6)**

---

*Jewish Ancestors?*

## A Guide to Jewish Genealogy in Latvia & Estonia

ISBN: 0-9537669-9-3/ISBN: 978-0-9537669-9-4

**Arlene Beare**

◆ Points you in the right direction for researching your roots in both the UK and in Latvia & Estonia◆
◆An insight into a host of available records◆
◆Useful tips and information for the genealogical traveller to this area◆

**Price: £5.95 + 80p p&p (US$16)**

---

*Jewish Ancestors?*

## A Guide to Organising Your Family History Records

ISBN: 09537669-4-2/ISBN: 978-0-9537669-4-9

**Rosemary Wenzerul**

◆If your papers are in a mess then this book is for you◆
◆Are your records suitably preserved for future generations? ◆
◆Up to date information about new technology◆
◆Hundreds of ideas to help you◆

**Price: £4.95 +80p p&p (US$13)**